Some, like elephants

Some, like elephants

Laura Glen Louis

For Yalda

Fondly

[signature]

Aug 2010

El León Literary Arts
BERKELEY

"An Exacting Man" was delivered in different form at the
Memorial for Alfred Peet, in October, 2007, and was first
published as a broadside by Peet's Coffee & Tea, 2008.

El León Literary Arts is a private foundation established to extend the
array of voices essential to a democracy's arts and education.

El León Literary Arts is distributed by
Small Press Distribution, Inc.
800-869-7553
www.spdbooks.org

El León books are also available on Amazon.com

El León website: www.elleonliteraryarts.org

Publisher: Thomas Farber
Managing editor: Kit Duane
Cover photos: Laura Glen Louis
Cover design: Judy July
Text design: Sara Glaser

ISBN 978-0-9795285-4-5

for
the living

foreword

An Attempt

I'd not lived till I'd felt the singe
of Death's hot breath as He rushed past
Were His touch not so chill a hover
I'd have sworn He was my lover

Speak for the dead, and from the fringe?
Who am I to steel this beat?
Wails peal the air. Do you not hear?
Here, take my style, my seat

Sonnet has quatrains, a couplet chaser
Pantoum do-si-dos in its repeat
Abecedarius orders the various
Two-three-two dance haiku feet

But elegy and lament
—these jet jewels—
have no set arrangement.
For honoring the dead there are no rules

How dare I write of the day
they died, or the way?
Or, the moment they had to know it?
Sterling scouts, they went before
If their loss did not intelligence give
why then did we send them forth?

elegies

Alight

Ken Durling 1952–2007

You think you have time
Half of spring break remains
from students sublime
and teaching's give and take
    here, in Shasta's eden

You boogie to polyphony
Tits, terns, hundreds of birds
No—hundreds of *species*
Cinnamon teal, patchwork loons
Chick-chick-chickadee
Kite, coot, Canada goose
    So much lift gifts you

You take sax to lips
to Bebop tunes
Birds turn as you land
There—knee deep in water
A genuine man!
They call / you answer
You tweet / they toot, and wonder
what rare creature
would wear your feather

Cow wanders, seeking,
like you, a greener green
Red hawk slips and slacks
in currents warm, unseen
You've flown, known
convection, conduction,
faith—forces invisible
except for their trace

    A singular day
You sketched a pavane
You were the bomb
You sang the aspens
Riffed with ravens. Caught
on film the soul of migration
Let your mind wander
farther than could feet
    Egret unfurls. Water
drips off the cape of wings

    Twilight
You drift on down the road
Hawk flashes, returns
You yearn to fly with him
as brother, as other
Sun's low, the light golden
    You turn—
—miss seeing the cow
Black. Bovine. Dumb as destiny

After the crash nothing cohered
Nouns and verbs were numb
Conjunctions, left hanging

~

If sense and solace
be made of randomness
Random this:
You came for the birds
The birds came for you
　　Below the hawk
one other sent,
low and sleek,
wings folded arrow,
short curved beak
flew swift and low
and drew your view
like a mother, who,
seeing the Reaper
drive the scythe,
turned her son
to point his view to one
of flighted beauty

Five Crowded in an Office
Lee Wai Chung 1909–1983

Five crowded in an office
Six, if you counted the doctor
Lung cancer, he said. In the outer office
Mother, non-smoker. Still brunette

Rare, the doctor began. How rare?
Cantonese. Woman. Non-smoker. Emigrant.
Bio-experiment? Loss of home, its very scent?
Her cells ran amok, yet here she was, still innocent

Her doll hands could sew a dress
caress my head, wring chicken's neck,
The healer cleared his throat, our cousin
(Nor could it have been easy for him)

Emigrants all, we triaged
though pierced by the same dart:
Had any of us, each born in a different town,
ever lived in such an eminent Canton?

How my brothers and I avoided the clarity
of our sister who childhooded in that killer
before the rest of us were a glimmer
Father too, though his smoking was a rarity

My family shifted. They'd heard plenty
But I, naive, greedy as Pandora, I leaned
Our cousin had explored inside our mother
and sobered by the reconnoiter

now dared, *A year* (in which I heard: *Less*)
Then he asked who would tell her, his auntie
Too late I recalled the feint when pressed
by the interrogator: Think. Don't blink.

As Newton's laws of motion ever must apply,
their downcast eyes tipped my balance: I rose,
thinking that as the youngest and childless, I,
in naming Death's desire, might have had less to lose

Every chance to speak I dismissed as lacking
when it was the envoy who was the fool
She had trusted me to deliver, and for that
my silence gave false hope. Was more cruel

As for the delivery, it was a disaster
Two crypts, a choice, a view, I blurted
with all the cowardice of a drive-by shoot.
English, I used, words on which she hung,
leaving her to decipher this mystery in any tongue

An Exacting Man
Alfred Peet, 1920–2007

Young and of a culture that revered Zen
and our elders, I called you Mister Peet,
especially when you suffered no fools with screed.
The flagship on Vine we called the opium den.
People lined up before we opened,
14 oz mugs and Alladins in hand.
Many a day I couldn't abide the heat,
the beans, the beans, Major D, Garuda blend,
oil slicking the mounds in bins,
the whine of blades pulverizing beans,
of beans scooped from the bins,
the thousand tinkles raining on the scales,
the steam hisses. An assault on the senses.
Or—music.
Aromatic bliss.
A smell you could taste on lips.

Keith arrived, driver/roaster. Interloper in the seraglio!
Delly at the counter fresh as hope, skirting aproned Anna,
freckled Jill, Liz, ever constant, Nut/Meg, and, ah—Bibiana,
all *French Vogue* and *Harper's BAZAAR*. But, Marsha
with the bedroom eyes, Marsha, you put at the bar.

Day one, you slid over a card. I signed in pen,
gaining access to your dollars, your float.
I wondered, aloud, how far I could go
on fifty grand (and had you for a moment).
You taught me to juggle income and outgo,
admonished me never be late with the payroll,
but mostly I was hired to listen.
No light shone between our desks
but there were days when I wished
to push my oak monster out to the street
and leave you to rant in peace, Mister Peet.
The woman who bedded her daughter's ex-beau
filled mail orders and shared our space, but not your woes.
You made me confidante. Difficult treasure, yet
I guarded your secrets. Then burned the map when I left.

Tastings took place at six while the town slept.
The senses needed stillness, a calm aspect.
You donned lab coat, courting art and alchemy,
lined up French press pots, porcelain cups, three.
Starting left, you slurped the brown-black
You chewed and gargled, then spat
and declared the coffee's pedigree.
How does one get to be so exacting?

Dinner, my house: hearing some lieder
you, guessing the soprano, poked the air and blared,
"Elly Ameling! That woman has no soul!"
I shrank, lest you might track with those
same discriminate eyes and also find me lacking.

You were a hard nut, Mister Peet.
But, you were also sweet of heart in a hairshirt glove.
I found a lump, you phoned a friend,
got a surgeon, like *that*. Some kind of thinking of.
Every other month, my fellow immigrant,
you at Red Cross rolled up your sleeve
and with regularity worthy of a penitent
gave back blood for the countrymen of liberators
at whose feet ... thank God ... freed
from Nazi toil but not the deeds.
The rest unsaid. Unpayable.

Exacting man. But, you were hard taught.
In youth, from you, was much exacted.

The Burden of Wings

Agnes 1984–2005

1

She came skittering across the road like a waterbird
some massive-winged creature on impossible legs
What use, legs? She was built for soaring

Brunch was arranged
the way dawn was arranged, and the dusk
The sun behind her the paler star

We fell on one another like long lost kin
Her harp/my piano, my cloth/her clay
And know it was I who ate *her* dust

But—who was that sitting with us
in the red vinyl booth, still looking sharp?
Oh, yes—her father/my friend, thrilled catalyst,

who wanted her to glimpse a former him, a former us,
who wanted me to know her porcelain qualities
Though he gave no hint of any dualities

She founded a mission (at twenty)
Taught civics—in Spanish, with ease
"She out-hiked *me* in the Tetons," said the father/jock

Bewitched, I never thought to play the whole jukebox:
Signed, Sealed, Delivered. He Ain't Heavy, He's my Brother
We could have danced the spoons, sang one another

How we subverted the schedule, yet the day too fleet
for the thousand queries that follow the reveal;
or, for wallowing among the willow;

for conjuring her dad leaning out the bricked window;
for baking together, or happenstance
For reciting "all ye need to know"

Look, we wore the same size glove
Both made things with our hands, for love
    Found self in silence, and solace at the fount

2

Six feet the covered bed
Six feet thick her blanket of moss
Six feet tall the six who shouldered her to rest

A twist of leaf fluttered from the branch
The mother faltered
The father lent his resolve

A thousand descended, bearing savory meats and sweet
Six feet from fingertip to tip, their embrace
Six feet, the fathom

At fifteen fathoms a diver is as if drunk. At forty, she loses all reason
So deep had she plunged that the thousand keening at the breach
linked hand to hand, still could not reach her

Measure her sterling talents
against her artful struggle for balance
no more visible than the blood in a ballerina's slipper

Her sister lingered under the linden, braving gusts and the siren
Her brother flung a dense rubber ball the size of his heart
hitting, hitting, hitting the wall till his stick flew apart

Her mother drifted in the girl's room, caressed her things,
opened this book and that, savoring
any word in the margin

Downstairs, that dry night, her father slipped into the den
and arranged to gather his family closer
to the equator

3

    Ash
her harp, tall as a father, just as constant
She needed to feel. She felt too much

She pulled harp to breast to beg an ode to clarity,
imploring Euterpe to counterpoint a plea
nothing short of vain

Outside, the autumn sun set the air afire
and revealed a truth so dire
it hurt her teeth. Peace?

At five, her sleeps were goodnight tunes and sugar tarts
At fifteen, she nailed stick shift's uphill start (in reverse)
Her father leaned: *Now you can do anything*

But, as does the star, even able wanes
She staggered. Who would not
under the burden of wings?

The sun so pregnant it seemed to be bleeding
As did the bullet, and the instrument
She stilled till she could imagine succeeding

As for the day it, too, was innocent

4

Thousand Cranes, the shop was called
Thousand Cranes, those birds of honor

Fold, bend
colored squares
six by six by six by six
A thousand folds, a thousand bends
A thousand more, a thousand cranes

Sadako Sasaki, at two, her city, bombed.
At twelve, leukemia's bride

Fold, bend
colored squares
six by six by six by six
A thousand folds, a thousand bends
A thousand more, a thousand cranes

A thousand cranes to beg one wish:
Heal my body. Make me whole

I turned my back. The seduction was swift
Ikat silk indigo blue. Sea grass! *Raku!* Oh, this!
Oh this! *Shikibuton!* What was amiss?
Out came her wallet, for her non-yet apartment
Silk! What would her mother think?
(Now? I'd give anything)

Fold, bend
a paper square, a standing bird
A thousand folds, a thousand bends
A thousand bends, a thousand cranes
A thousand cranes, a granted wish:
Rescue from ailments grave. So legend says

Fold, bend
Hope, solace
Temporary shelter for restless hands
A thousand folds, a thousand bends
A thousand more, a thousand cranes
A thousand cranes, a thousand flights

I know how to fold the crane. I
could have easily taught her

Some, like elephants

Some slash the sky
with fighter kites
Oblivious to the graces

Some walk from town to town
seeking, then skirting,
all those old familiar places

Some, worn down
from years of ass-wiping
are crushed by what dies with the dying:

the voice of reason, the unassuming wit,
their own younger selves that inspired it
The sweet undoing. The thriving

Some build shrines for their misery
Museum a house of Mother-stuff
into what was to be the nursery

Some cut the lawn on hands and knees—
Some don't eat, shave, bathe, but read and read—
Some tamp it all the way down so the kids don't see

Some, like elephants, circle the ground
They sniff every inch the downed, and glean.
As for bone or ivory

they pass it all around, like ash,
each looking one to the next
while holding in his hands the dead

Some grab in the hall their wives' best friends
while wife beds Morpheus and descends,
each breath a mighty labor as lungs fill again with fluid

After the cancer is done and gone (call it murder/suicide)
he roams and roams, finding no woman's eyes as wide
No woman ever as fluid

Some remarry with rude speed
Leaving even adult children twice bereaved
For mourning, they have much more time

Some are doing, thank you, just fine.

The artist applies paint to canvas, and to paper, ink
working quickly, not letting himself think
as he tries to capture in the dying something lasting

The lucky dare to laugh
Stare down their bald selves in the glass
Ask, *Who loves ya, baby?*

Some rage at the moon,
At blinding noon
Night and day, their TV blasting

Some can't bear to delete even the mundane
Please get milk and eggs
I'll be home soon

ruminations

The hour of the stone

My own demise?
An uneventful life
Nearly this, nearly that
Nearly run over, twice
Nearly stepped off a mountain
Rear-ended twice and twice broadsided
Choked (more than once) on rice
and the pool. A swallow sufficed
as one element invaded another's

room. Tiny—
what can be our undoing. Micro-
scopic. Voracious cells. Pernicious.
Tenacious. Pugnacious little
thugs. Four young men
sauntered into my store
Bolted the door. In my ribbons
they had no interest. Nor
in my notions

Death's a tease
planning something random
for me and will make it
appear wholly
my folly. Yes,
I could die of inattention
Many do

Career Day,
   inner city teen: —So,
how long you plan on doing this
   writing thing? —Till the day I die.
      —Oooh. *Good* answer, he said
seeing work anew. Die
   writing. Die

      laughing. Die shaking my booty
   to Stravinsky and Chopin. Die
in my garden, watching agave
   calve. Die recalling son chirp
      a chirp heard to round my world
whenever I returned from singing:
   "Second dinner?"

      Death could hook His crusty finger
   make me last but feeble, yet
alert as Salieri to the wasting
   while I cannot
      for the death of me
think
   or remember the word for it

Johnny promised a His & Her Rockefeller
   but it was us that died. Just
as well. No future (nor any present)
   with a man who isn't
      his word. —I jest
because, to ensure, one would never
   get out of beds

      Been assaulted.
   Stalked.
Heart stopped. Three
   tick-less seconds.
Mother tried to kill me once
   I see now it was self-defense
      As an embryo, I was formidable.
Full of potential. A stone. She didn't know
   Death had other plans

      I was five, the stranger, burly
   My family? Sea sick
Crossing the Pacific
   Want to see? He lifted me,
sat me on the rail.
   My skirt flapped, his nose smoked
      Fast, the ocean, far below. He
taught me trust by letting go
   And catching. Letting go. And laughing

Sixteen,
  nearly stepped into the path
of a MACK, walking
   while reading Abe Kōbō
     Ah — to be undone by truth
and beauty (Really,
  not a bad way to go)

    But, of the vast array
   let me not die from a lack
of heart, or of a failure to communicate
   And, please, let me not die
     of suspense. Die conjuring, yes,
more present tense. At least say
      I died trying

Acknowledgments

Unstinting in their offerings, I thank

Thomas Farber, a prince among men, for the gift of enduring friendship; Jim Krusoe, for his reflection and encouragement; Norman Glendenning, who makes possible the writing life; Nathan Glendenning, for showing me the way;

for ongoing dialog, and for invitations to speak where many of these poems found first audience, Randall Babtkis & New College, Buddy Born, Ronni Brega, Martha Cook, Jane Downs, Rachel Durling, Michel Fondbertasse, Amy Gottlieb, Christiane Khan, Peter and Susan Lindh, Larry London, Liz O'Connell-Gates, Jim Reynolds, Ruth Reynolds, Diana Rowen, Elizabeth Walukas;

and these donors whose generosity and gifts-in-kind made this chapbook a reality: Heather Bloch, Buddy Born, Ronni Brega, Ann Callaway, Tess Clark, Martha Cook, Ian Crane, Kit Duane, Thomas Farber, Norman Glendenning, Amy Gottlieb, Edith Kasin, Jen Louis, Hedley and Ilona Louis, Ray Louis and Elizabeth Walukas, Ruth and Jim Reynolds, Tracy Washington (in honor of Etta and Brock), Ellen and Robert Wong, and Andrea Young.

Author of *Talking in the Dark,* a Barnes & Noble
Discover book, and recipient of the
Katherine Anne Porter Prize for short fiction,
Laura Glen Louis has had work included
in *Best American Short Stories.*

Visit www.lauraglenlouis.com